Best of Friends

The Girls' Ultimate Guide to Friendship

BY SHERRY CHIGER

Scholastic Inc.
New York Toronto London Auckland Sydney
Mexico City New Delhi Hong Kong

ISBN 0-439-18760-5

Copyright © 2000 by Scholastic Inc.
Cover photo © Myrleen Ferguson, PhotoEdit
Designed by Peggy Gardner

12 11 10 9 8 7 6 5 4 3 2 1   0 1 2 3 4 5/0

Printed in the U.S.A.
First Scholastic printing, November 2000

Table of Contents

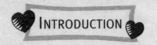

All About Friends

O ne of the best feelings in the world is hanging out with a friend. It doesn't matter what you're doing — whether it's dancing, giggling, swimming, snacking, or even working on homework. It can all be more fun if you're doing it with a bud.

Because friends are so wonderful, this entire book is about friendships. You'll read about how to meet friends, how to get to know them better, and how to stay friends forever. You'll also be able to take some fun friend quizzes to learn more about yourself and your buds, and get some ideas on great friendship stuff you can make for a friend. Best of all, this book is a guide that you'll be able to refer to again and again, throughout your many friendships.

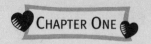

CHAPTER ONE

Making Friends

You can never have too many friends. That's one of the great things about friendships: No matter how many you have, there's always room for more!

But some people find it easier to make friends than others do. For instance, if you're shy, you probably find it tough to walk up to a new girl at school and just start talking. Then again, if you *are* the new girl in school, the idea of greeting a roomful of strangers is bound to make you jittery, no matter how outgoing you are.

The fact is there's no single best way to make new friends. Different ways work better for different people. To find out which ways may work best for you, take the following quiz.

What's Your Friend-Making Style?

Answer the following questions true (T) or false (F).

1. I often raise my hand to read out loud or make a presentation in class.

    T_____   F_____

2. If a new girl moves into the neighborhood, I will say hi to her, even if I don't know her.

    T_____   F_____

3. I've known most of my friends all my life.

    T_____   F_____

4. I'd rather play team games, like soccer or kickball, than one-on-one games, like jacks.

    T_____   F_____

5. I don't like being chosen to be a team captain.

    T_____   F_____

6. Most of my friends are very similar to me (for example, we're in

the same dance class or live on the same block).

T_____   F_____

Score
1. T=2 points   F=1 point
2. T=2 points   F=1 point
3. T=1 point   F=2 points
4. T=2 points   F=1 point
5. T=1 point   F=2 points
6. T=1 point   F=2 points

If you scored 8 or more points, you're a "people person." You love hanging out with lots of friends. You're probably adventurous, too — chances are you like trying new things and joining all sorts of clubs and teams.

In fact, joining clubs and teams is a great way to make more friends. Try taking up an activity that's new to you. For example, if you already play on your neighborhood soccer and softball teams, try something that's not sports-related, such as a dance class or choir. That way, you're bound to meet girls who may be different from your other friends and with whom you can share all sorts of new experiences. Besides, you may just discover a hidden talent or two while you're at it!

If you scored fewer than 8 points, you probably prefer having a few close friends. You may find it's not easy to make the first move and strike up a conversation with a girl you don't know very well. This is not at all unusual, however. Lots of people of all ages find it tough to break the ice.

Taking part in a group activity that you enjoy can help you meet other kids. Do you love to draw? Then why not ask your parents if you can take art lessons at the local community center? Do you like to write? Then why not work on your school newspaper? The other kids that take part in these activities are there for the same reason as you — because they enjoy doing those things. So, you already have something in common with them!

You might also find it easier to make friends when you're with a smaller group than a larger group, which can be overwhelming to people. For instance, if you have a choice between joining two Girl Scout troops, you might want to sign up with the one that has fewer girls.

Of course, sometimes you're bound to find yourself with a bunch of kids you don't know. Let's say you're at a birthday party, and the only person you know is the girl who invited you. Everyone else seems to be chattering in groups of three or four. There's no way you can bring yourself to walk up to one of those groups and say hello. Not true! Take a deep breath, walk over to a couple of girls, and introduce yourself. You'll be glad you did — and so will they!

What Should I Say?

Even if you find it super simple to walk up to a girl you don't know and introduce yourself, you might not find it so easy to know what to say next. Learning how to start a conversation, and a friendship, is a skill, just like reading. Some people seem to pick it up easily. Others get off to a slow start. But eventually everyone can learn how to read — or how to start a conversation.

Here are a few tips:

✔ *Give a compliment.* Who doesn't love hearing nice things about themselves? "That's a cool notebook" or "I really like that diorama you did for your science project" is sure to get the conversation going. But don't flatter someone just to make them like you. If you think a girl's new shoes are kind of ugly, don't go on about how much you love them. People can tell when a compliment is fake. Instead, praise something else that you really do admire.

✔ **Ask a question.** This is the perfect follow-up to a compliment. After you say how cool her notebook is, ask where she got it. Or after you praise her diorama, ask how she made it. If you're at a birthday party, you can ask how she knows the guest of honor.

✔ **Ask for help.** Doesn't it make you feel good when someone comes to you for advice or to ask your opinion? Why not make someone else feel good, then? Your request can be as simple as "Can you help me reach that top shelf?" But, just as when you give a compliment, be honest. If you're already an ace at spelling, don't ask for help in studying for a spelling test.

✔ **Offer help.** If someone is struggling to carry a lunch tray and a pile of books, ask if you can lend a hand. If

the new girl in class looks lost, see if
she needs directions.

Don't Judge a Book by Its Cover

You've probably heard this expression. It
means don't judge someone by how she looks.
Just because a girl doesn't dress as cool as you
and your friends, or has an old-fashioned
hairstyle, or is heavier or skinnier or darker or
paler than you, doesn't mean she can't be lots
of fun and a great friend. If you refuse to make
friends with girls who are different from you,
you could be missing out on some terrific
adventures and fabulous times!

CHAPTER TWO

A Club of Your Own

One way to make new friends and have fun with your old friends is to form a club. Starting a club can be as much fun as belonging to one that already exists!

What's It All About?

Your club should have some sort of purpose. What hobbies or interests do you and your friends share? If you really like making beaded bracelets, that could be the theme of your club: You and other girls can get together to form a bracelet-making club. Or if you love reading the Harry Potter books, form a book club in which you and your pals talk about the stories.

Here are a few other ideas for clubs:

❀ *Collecting clubs:* Do you collect trading cards, Beanie Babies, or posters and pictures of your favorite celebs? Whatever it is you collect, chances are good that other kids collect the same things, too.

❀ *Fan clubs:* Are your walls covered with photos of Mia Hamm and other soccer players? Have you seen every episode of your favorite TV show? Then why not form a club where you can talk about them!

❀ *Activity clubs:* If you sometimes have trouble finding other kids to play Monopoly or double Dutch with, forming a club can fix that!

❀ *Volunteer clubs:* All sorts of organizations need donations of stuff, from money to old eyeglasses. You can help by forming a club to collect whatever it is these organizations need. To find a worthy cause you'd like to collect for, ask your teachers or parents for suggestions.

Getting Members

To get kids to join your club, you can simply walk up to them and ask if they're interested. But a more fun way is to write up "membership passes." At the top of a piece of paper, write something like, "*This pass is good for one membership into a brand-new, top secret club. Come learn all about it."* You can drop a few hints about the club if you want — maybe glue a few beads to each pass if you're forming a jewelry-making club, or just come right out and say what the purpose of the club is. Then write the time and the place to meet, and sign your name.

Four to six members is a good number for a club. If you have too many kids, you may find it tough to get everyone to agree on anything. For a fun mix of members, invite some friends you've known for a long time and others you haven't known long at all, or invite girls who you don't really know but think would be fun to spend time with.

The First Meeting

Once everyone is together, you'll want to decide on things like a name for the club, how often and when you'll meet, and what meetings will be like. It also helps to have a club president. This person isn't the boss of the club. Instead, she keeps count whenever you have to vote on something and keeps order if members start to squabble.

You may think that because the club is your idea you should be president. You're much better off having everyone vote for a president, though. If you just elect yourself president, the others won't think it's fair, and they may end up quitting the club before it even gets started. But that doesn't mean you can't nominate yourself as a candidate for president!

Other things to vote on include the club name, the best time and place to meet, and if there are going to be any special rules. For example, maybe you want to vote on whether everyone should pitch in some money to buy a snack for each meeting.

Another thing to consider is how secret you want the club to be. Secret nicknames and handshakes can be a lot of fun. The same goes for a secret language. Do you know pig Latin? That's when you don't pronounce the first consonant of a word, but instead add it onto the end of the word, followed by "ay." The sentence "Let's meet tomorrow at noon" translates to "Ets-lay eet-may omorrow-tay at oon-nay." If that's not secret enough for you, put your own spin on pig Latin: You can change the last syllables instead, or come up with your own secret code.

Why Clubs Flop

Sometimes, after a few meetings, a club will suddenly flop. People drop out, or start bickering, and then no one is showing up anymore. Here are some reasons a club might fall apart, and how to prevent it from happening.

Problem: Meeting too frequently.

Solution: Given how busy everyone is, it's almost impossible to schedule meetings for more than once a week (and sometimes for every week). And even if you and the other members have voted on when and where to meet, be flexible. During spring vacation, for instance, you may have to skip a week if some members are going away with their families.

Problem: Not meeting often enough.

Solution: If you get together only once a month, so much time will pass between meetings that other things might attract your attention instead. This is easy to fix, though: Just try to meet at least twice a month.

Problem: Never getting anything done.

Solution: Sometimes goofing around is fun. But if you and the other club members want to achieve certain goals, you need to set an agenda, or schedule, for your meetings and stick to it. At the end of each meeting, set aside a few minutes to vote on the agenda for the next one.

Problem: Too many rules.

Solution: Rules are important, because without them, nothing would get done. But let's face it, we all have tons of rules we have to deal with in school and at home. So if you insist on too many rules in your club, it won't be much fun. If members begin complaining about a rule or ignoring it, you should think about changing or getting rid of that particular rule.

Don't Be a Brat!

Part of the fun of a club is that it's something you share with only a small group of kids. And if things go well with the club, you're probably going to be talking about it at school. But don't be a brat about it by purposely talking about it to girls you don't want as members.

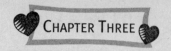

CHAPTER THREE

Being Friends

For some people, making friends is easier than being friends. They might have a new best friend every year, or even every month. They can strike up a friendship just by talking to someone at a party or while playing catch at the park, but then the next thing you know, they aren't hanging around with that girl anymore.

Lots of kids think that being friends is so simple, they don't have to make an effort. But that's not true. To be friends with someone, you sometimes have to overlook habits of theirs that may annoy you. You also have to realize that you can't always get your own way. But while being a friend takes a bit of work, it's almost always worth it!

What's Your Friendship Style?

Everyone has different views on how a friendship should work. Some people think friends should share everything. Some people prefer to do things with a group of friends rather than with only one best friend.

This quiz will help you discover your friendship style.

1. When playing a game like jacks, I like to play with:
   a) my best friend and maybe one other girl.
   b) whoever wants to, so long as we play by my rules.
   c) as many friends who want to play.

2. If my best friends don't like the new girl in class, even though she seemed nice when I talked with her, I:
   a) invite her to join us at recess anyway.
   b) stop liking her, too.
   c) am nice to her, but only when my other friends aren't around.

3. I get annoyed when:
   a) my best friend decides to try a new sport, like joining a soccer team, without me.
   b) my best friend insists that I

join the soccer team with her, even though I don't like soccer.

4. When I make a new friend, I:
   a) always introduce her to my other friends.
   b) like to keep her away from my other friends, in case she likes them better than she likes me.

5. If I'm out with a friend and we run into a friend of hers who I don't know, I:
   a) introduce myself and ask if she would like to join us.
   b) don't care if she joins us or not.
   c) try to get my friend to say good-bye so that we can continue doing what we were doing, just the two of us.

6. If a girl I don't like invites my friend to a party, I:
   a) tell my friend that if she goes to the party, she can't be my friend anymore.

b) try to get myself invited to the party, too.

c) feel bad, but think of something else to do that day instead.

Score

1. a) 1   b) 5   c) 3
2. a) 5   b) 1   c) 3
3. a) 1   b) 5
4. a) 5   b) 1
5. a) 3   b) 5   c) 1
6. a) 1   b) 3   c) 5

If you scored 5 to 9 points, you tend to be a possessive friend. You are probably afraid that if you don't spend as much time as possible with someone, she will find someone that she likes better than you. But the truth is, if you insist on hogging all of your friend's time, she will probably start to resent it, and then she just might begin to like you less than she used to. If someone truly likes you, she will make a point of spending time with you — you don't have to force her to do it. You can't make someone like you or be your friend.

If you scored 10 to 25 points, you are a fairly typical friend. Sometimes you like to spend lots of time with your buds, but sometimes you enjoy going off on your own. You may get a little jealous if your best friend seems to be spending a lot of time with someone else, but it doesn't happen often, or you have other friends you can hang out with instead. And while what your friends think is important to you, you don't let it rule your life. What a cool friend you are!

If you scored 26 to 30 points, you are an independent friend. No one will ever accuse you of being too pushy or clingy. But if you are *too* independent, it could be because you aren't willing to compromise; it's either your way or the highway. And while spending time by yourself can be wonderful, you'll want to be careful not to miss out on sharing experiences and feelings with others. If that means sometimes agreeing to play a game that you're not crazy about, you should make the effort anyway. After all, the more friends you get to know, the more you'll realize that it's impossible to get your own way all the time!

Do You Recognize These Friends?

Do any of the fictional friends described below sound familiar? Maybe they remind you of someone you know — or maybe yourself?

CLINGY CLARISSA

"Can I come, too?" is one of her favorite expressions. If one of her buds is going somewhere (even if it's just to the bathroom during recess!), doing something, or talking to someone else, Clarissa has to be involved.

What to do if she's a friend of yours: Tell her that you like doing things with her, but just not everything. If she tries to be included on an afternoon date that you were planning to spend with another friend, very nicely say, "I'm sorry, but Emily and I had planned to spend today with just the two of us. But why don't you and I get together Friday instead?"

What to do if (gulp!) she's you: Back off a little bit. If you give your pals a chance to miss you, then they'll probably be more eager than ever to ask you to join them. In the meantime, try to meet new friends, so that you're not always anxious about doing things with the friends you have.

FICKLE FIONA

One week she's a girl's best bud. Every day after school, she has some fantastic plans for her most recent pal. Then, two weeks later,

Fiona is skipping down the hall at school with a *new* best bud, making all sorts of fantastic plans with her. Worse, she barely says hi to the girl who was her best friend for the previous two weeks.

What to do if she's a friend of yours: You could try to ask Fiona why she no longer wants to do anything with you. Perhaps you said or did something that made her angry. But if Fiona has done this sort of thing before with other friends, you're best off realizing that it's Fiona who can't keep a friend — not you.

What to do if (oh, no!) she's you: If you feel the need to make new best friends on a regular basis, you should ask yourself why. Do you get bored easily with people? If that's the case, you might want to make more than one friend at a time. Try joining a club or getting involved with a sport or other group activity. Do you feel disappointed or let down by people once you get to know them? If so, your expectations may be too high — after all, nobody's perfect. Do you constantly like to make new friends? That's great — don't ever stop. But when you make a new friend, don't drop your old ones. Make a point of spending time with your older friends as well as your newer ones.

She doesn't mean to tell everyone what to do — it's just that she is 100-percent certain that her way is the right way! Whether it's how to play Monopoly or how her friends should wear their hair, Bernadette knows best, and she feels it's her duty as a friend to share her knowledge with her pals!

What to do if she's a friend of yours: If you don't agree with her, don't be afraid to tell her, nicely. Don't say: "You are so wrong, Bernadette. In fact, you're always wrong!" Instead, try, "I don't think you're right about that. Do you want to ask someone else to see which one of us is correct?" If she continues to insist that she's right (even when you know she's wrong), you have to decide how important it is to you to let her have her own way or to stand up for yourself. But if you find that she is almost always having her own way, you should tell her — especially if you no longer want to hang out with her because of that.

What to do if (horrors!) she's you: Over the course of a week, keep count of how many

23

times you say things like "But my way is better" or "Either we play my way or I'm not playing at all." If it's a lot of times, ask yourself how important it is that you get your own way. For instance, is it really worth making a big deal because your friends want to play hopscotch and you'd rather play jump rope? Before you automatically start arguing your point, stop to think whether it's truly a point that's worth arguing!

EAGER ELEANOR

Eleanor wants to make everyone happy. If a friend is desperate for tickets to a women's soccer game, Eleanor says she can get them for her — even if she can't. If one of her pals gets angry because Eleanor can't live up to one of her many promises, Eleanor will try to make it up by giving the pal her favorite hairband and her lunch snacks for a week.

What to do if she's a friend of yours: It can be very tempting to take advantage of Eleanor. After all, she is so eager to be your friend that she's willing to do almost anything for you. But you need to be a good friend to her, too, by telling her to cool it. Let her know that while it's great to help out a friend, she doesn't need to "buy" friendships by con-

24

stantly doing favors or giving gifts. And if she does help you out sometimes, make sure to offer her a hand sometime in return.

What to do if (it can't be!) she's you: By constantly offering to do things for your friends, you're not giving them a chance to like you for being you. And if you keep promising things you can't deliver, they're not going to think of you as nice and helpful; instead, they'll view you as a fibber and unreliable. And that's not anybody's idea of a good friend!

Getting to Know You

Friendship is funny sometimes. You can be friends with someone for years and not even know her middle name. And then other times, you can meet someone and within a week know all about her family, her nosy next-door neighbor, how she wants to be a trapeze artist when she's older, and why she's afraid of bees!

If you want to see how well you know a friend, jot down the answers to the following questions, then have her mark how many answers you got correct. Then the two of you can swap — let her answer the questions about you, and then check to see how many she answered correctly.

How Well Do You Know Her?

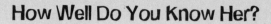

1. What's your friend's favorite color?
2. What is her fave food?
3. What food does she hate the most?
4. What's her favorite subject in school?
5. Who's her favorite performer?
6. What does she want to be when she gets older?
7. If she could meet one fictional character, who would it be?
8. When is her birthday?
9. What is she most afraid of?
10. If a genie granted her three wishes, what would she wish for?
11. If she could trade places with someone for a day, who would it be?
12. What was the happiest day of her life?
13. What makes her sad?
14. What makes her angry?
15. What makes her laugh?

Of course, the more questions you answer correctly, the better you know your friend. But if you don't get very many answers correct, that doesn't mean you aren't good friends. It simply means that you still have plenty to learn about each other — and that can be loads of fun.

Here are a few other ways to get to know each other better:

✔ *Interview each other.* Pretend you're a famous reporter or TV talk-show host and that your friend is someone you're interviewing for the first time. Then trade places and have her interview you.

✔ *Play the "desert island" game.* A famous radio program in England asks celebrities what they would bring to a desert island. You and your friend can answer the same type of questions. Decide what books, games, and household items each of you would bring along.

✔ *Make self-portrait collages.* Not only is this a good way to get to know each other better, but it's a great rainy-day activity, too! Get a bunch of magazines that you and your family have already read, and cut out all sorts of pictures and words that you think best describe you. They may be photos of things you like, or they could be pictures of places you'd like to visit or things you'd like to do. Then paste the images and words in a collage. When the collages are done, swap yours with your friend's, and the two of you can talk about what each of you selected.

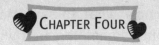

CHAPTER FOUR

Friends Help Each Other

Being a friend isn't all fun and games. Being a good friend sometimes means helping a pal get through tough times, too. Then again, having a good friend means that if you're going through a rough patch, you don't have to suffer through it alone — your friend will be there to help you, just as you are there to help her.

Being There for Her

If your friend's folks are getting a divorce, or her pet dog died, or one of her parents is out of work, she's bound to be sad or angry — or maybe both at the same time. She's also not likely to be as much fun as she usually is. But that doesn't mean you should stop spending time with her. Chances are she needs you just as much, if not more, than when everything was going great.

It can also be hard for you when your friend is going through tough times. You might not know what to say. Maybe you're afraid of doing something that will make her feel worse. And if she's cranky or moping, you may even lose patience with her, making both of you feel worse.

Here are a few tips for helping a friend when times are tough:

✔ *Ask how she's doing.* This can be really difficult, but it's really important, too. It used to be that friends never brought up troubling subjects, such as an illness or a death in the family. They thought that by talking about the subject, they would make the person feel worse. But that's not true. If someone in your friend's family is sick or has died, she's already feeling bad. Knowing that you care enough to ask about her and her situation will make her feel a little better.

✔ *Ask if she wants to talk about it.* Don't pester her with detailed questions. Instead, say something like, "If you want to talk, I'm here to listen." If your friend says no thanks, remind her that if she changes her mind in the future she can always come to you.

✔ **Listen.** This seems obvious, but a lot of people think they're listening when they're really offering advice. Let's say your friend is crying because her cat, Fluffy, was run over by a car and died. Telling her that she can always get another cat isn't going to make her feel better — right now she doesn't want another cat; she wants Fluffy. Instead, simply listen to her. When she talks about how soft and friendly Fluffy was, you can say, "Yes, he was." Don't try to fix the situation; you can't. The best thing you can do is let her express her feelings.

✔ **Don't blab.** If your friend is telling you, and only you, that her parents are splitting up, don't tell your other buds. It's obvious that she trusts you. The last thing she needs now is for you to betray that trust.

✔ **Be patient.** Maybe last year you went through a bad situation similar to that of your friend, but you got over it much quicker. That doesn't mean your friend should be able to get over her situation in the same way and within the same amount of time. Every situation is slightly different, and every person is different, too. Besides, you may remember getting over a situation in a matter of days when in reality it took you much longer; sometimes we block out exactly how awful certain events were and how long they lasted. But if you're worried that your friend seems to be especially slow in accepting her situation, talk to a parent or a teacher. Your friend may need some outside help in dealing with the rough times.

Bringing Good Cheer

All friends need cheering up from time to time. Maybe your bud is going through tough times at home, or maybe she's upset about getting into a fight with her older sister. Whatever the reason, why not try one of these suggestions to help cheer her up?

☺ *Make her a card*. Draw some of her favorite things on it, or a picture of the two of you doing one of her favorite activities.

☺ *Give her a bouquet.* Flowers cheer up almost everyone! If you have a garden, ask your parents if you can pick a few flowers to give to your friend, then wrap the stems in yarn. If you don't have a garden or flowers aren't blooming yet, make your own bouquet with construction paper and crayons.

☺ *Let her be "queen for a day."* For one day, let your friend decide which games you'll play, what music you'll listen to together, or any other choices that need to be made.

☺ *Lend a hand.* If your friend is down because she could use some help — for instance, she's sad that she did poorly on a math test — offering some assistance could be the best way of cheering her up.

When You're the Friend Who's Down

The day may come when you're down in the dumps. There's nothing wrong with letting friends know that you're feeling down about

33

something. We all know people who moan and cry about every little thing. But some people are the exact opposite — even when something truly sad happens, they keep it to themselves. Maybe they're afraid that if they cry or complain, their friends won't like them as much.

But if you're keeping a problem to yourself because you're afraid of letting your friends see you upset, you're not giving your buds enough credit. Would you drop a friend because she'd confided in you? Of course not. If anything, you'd feel flattered that she trusted you and felt close enough to let you know what was bothering her.

You might think that a friend should notice if you're sad or upset and that she should ask you what's wrong. But she might not be that observant, or she might be wrapped up in her own thoughts. So feel free to confide in your close friends, especially if they've confided in you in the past. Being a friend means lending a sympathetic ear and a shoulder to cry on, and it also means allowing others to lend you a sympathetic ear and a shoulder to cry on, too.

CHAPTER FIVE

Good Friends, Not-So-Good Times

Wouldn't it be wonderful if you and your friends agreed on everything all the time, and you never argued about anything? Maybe it would be, but chances are you'll never find out — because all friends disagree from time to time.

Sometimes friends fight over silly things, like what to do on a rainy Saturday. Sometimes the fights are about more serious subjects — for instance, you trusted a friend with a secret, and she blabbed it to your entire class. And sometimes fights start out about something minor, such as which game to play, and end up being about something major, like whether one of you is way too bossy too much of the time.

Getting It Out in the Open

Lots of girls are afraid to let a friend know that they are angry about something she's done. They keep their feelings to themselves, all the time getting more and more angry inside, until they finally explode, yelling and shouting and confusing their friend, who didn't realize that anything was wrong.

If you're angry or upset with a friend, you should let her know what's bothering you. By dealing with it, you can prevent the matter from growing bigger and even more upsetting.

But there are right ways and wrong ways to tell a friend why you are angry or upset.

Wrong way: "You always have to get your own way! You're so bossy."

Right way: "We did things your way the last time, so let's do it my way this time."

Wrong way: "If you didn't have such a big mouth, I wouldn't have to be mad at you."

Right way: "I'm upset that you told

Charlotte the secret I told you not to tell anyone."

Wrong way: "You always pick on me! You're the meanest girl I know!"

Right way: "It hurts when you call me Klutzy Kelly. I'd like you to stop."

Fighting Fair

Once you tell a friend that you are upset with her, she may get upset right back. Then things can get messy, with all sorts of yelling and crying. That doesn't mean you should keep your complaints to yourself, though. But you should make sure that you fight fair.

What does it mean to "fight fair"? It means that there are certain rules you should follow when disagreeing with a friend.

Rule #1: Talk about the problem — but not about every little thing that she's ever done that has annoyed you. If you're upset because your friend lied to you about going away for the weekend, talk about that. But don't bring up the time two weeks ago when she accidentally tripped you, or how last year she was a half hour late meeting you at the playground after school!

Rule #2: No name-calling. It's fair to say, "I'm angry that you lied to me." It's not fair to say, "You're a big, fat, smelly liar."

Rule #3: Don't accuse her unless you know for a fact that she did something. If you're mad at Joanne because your friend Marissa told you that Joanne called you a crybaby behind your back, you shouldn't march up to Joanne and say, "I'm mad that you called me a crybaby." After all, Marissa could be wrong. Instead, say, "I heard that you called me a crybaby. Is that true?"

Rule #4: Keep calm. This can be really tough. But if you yell, your friend is probably going to yell, too, and then each of you will get louder and louder, and angrier and angrier, and that won't solve anything.

Rule #5: Listen to your friend's side of the story. Maybe your friend lied to you about going away for the weekend because her parents had forbidden her to tell anyone about their trip. Or maybe she did call you a crybaby behind your back, but now she's sorry and wants to apologize.

Rule #6: Don't get other friends involved. If you're angry with Zoe, tell Zoe. Don't tell all your other friends about it. Nothing good will come of it. Plus, your friends may end up feeling as if they have to choose sides—and they may not choose your side.

When You're in the Wrong

Nobody's perfect. That goes for your friends and for you. Maybe you're the one who lied to a friend, or called her names behind her back, or acted way too bossy. Now what?

When you know you're wrong, the best thing you can do is apologize. Even if your friend hasn't said anything to you about your lie or your name-calling, you should tell her you're sorry. It will prove to her what a good friend you are — and it's certain to make you feel better, too. You could also thank your friend for forgiving you and listening to you.

More Than a Simple Disagreement

Just because a friend apologizes, that doesn't mean you automatically have to forgive her and continue being her friend. Sometimes so-called friends really aren't good friends at all. If your friend makes you feel bad more than she makes you feel good, maybe the two of you weren't meant to be friends.

Sometimes you know in your gut when someone isn't acting like a good friend. Other times, though, it can be tough to tell. This quiz may help you decide whether someone is a good friend or not.

How Good a Friend Is She?

1. You and your mother had a big fight. When you tell your friend, she:
   a) interrupts you to tell you about a fight *she* had with *her* mother.
   b) listens to you.
   c) listens to you, then tells you to stop moping about it.

2. You won the class spelling bee! Your friend:

   a) congratulates you big-time.

   b) says, "That's great," then changes the subject to the time she won a swimming meet.

   c) asks if you cheated.

3. The last three times you and your friend played hopscotch, she insisted on going first. When you say you want to go first this time, she says:

   a) that she doesn't want to play anymore.

   b) sure.

4. The last time you told your friend a secret:

   a) she told one or two friends, but swore them to secrecy.

   b) she kept it to herself.

   c) are you kidding? You'd never trust this friend with a secret!

5. Once when your bud was over at your house, your older sister told her that people used to call you Sloppy Susan. You tell your friend how much you hate that nickname. She:

  a) promises never to tell a soul.
  b) calls you Sloppy Susan, but only when she's mad at you.
  c) tells the entire class about your nickname.

6. Oops! You said something really rotten to your friend. When you apologize, she:

  a) says she'll forgive you if you do her homework for a week.
  b) walks away and ignores you whenever you come by.
  c) says, "Okay. Let's forget it."

Score

  1. a) 5   b) 1   c) 3
  2. a) 1   b) 3   c) 5
  3. a) 5   b) 1
  4. a) 3   b) 1   c) 5
  5. a) 1   b) 3   c) 5
  6. a) 3   b) 5   c) 1

If your score is 5–8 points, you have yourself a great friend!

If your score is 9–18 points, your friend can sometimes be great, but other times she's not very loyal or trustworthy. Next time she does something that hurts you, like calling you a name you don't like or spilling the beans on a secret, tell her how much that upsets you. If she apologizes and makes an effort to improve, she may turn out to be an all-around great friend.

If your score is more than 18 points, your friend has probably done some things that have hurt you, and you may want to think about how close you want to be with her. If you usually have a lot of fun together, you might still want to do things with her, but perhaps you should think twice before trusting her with any secrets. But if you find that most of the time you are upset or angry with her, your best bet is to tell her when she does something that hurts you, and to spend more time with some of your other friends.

Growing Apart

If you're lucky, you and some of your buds will stay friends for years. But it's much more common for friends to grow apart over time. You may no longer enjoy doing the same things that one of your buds does, or vice versa. It doesn't mean that you and your friend are now enemies. It's just that the two of you may no longer want to spend so much time together.

You may feel sad if a friendship seems to be fading, especially if your friend is the one who seems to be growing apart from you. It's perfectly normal to feel bad about it. But keep in mind that many friendships change over time. What doesn't change is your memory of all the fun times you and your friend had. And keep in mind that since you were obviously able to become friendly with your onetime pal, you are certainly able to make new friends now and in the future!

CHAPTER SIX

Long-Distance Friendships

Most of your friends probably live nearby. If you don't go to school with them, you might see them regularly after school, like on your soccer team or in your Girl Scout troop. But sometimes friends move away, or maybe you're the one whose family moved to a new town. Just because you can no longer see your friends as often as you used to doesn't mean you can't still be close. What's more, thanks to pen pals and the Internet, you can even make friends with girls you'll never meet!

Moving Away but Staying Close

Staying close with a friend when you or she moves to another town or even another state can take a bit of extra work. After all, you can't just knock on her front door anymore when you want to see her, or phone her just to talk, because it costs more to telephone someone who lives far away. Also, each of you is likely to be making new friends and getting involved in new activities and interests that the other may know nothing about.

Fortunately, there are plenty of fun ways to help you and your long-distance friend stay in touch:

❀ *Say it in pictures.* You've probably heard the saying "A picture is worth a thousand words." Sometimes the best way to describe a special event, and to make a faraway friend feel involved in it, is by taking photographs and sending them to her. For example, if your bud is too far away to attend your birthday party, have your parents make extra copies of the photos of you and your party guests playing games and eating cake. Then mail them to your friend with captions explaining the action.

❀ *Record messages.* Sometimes there is nothing better than hearing a friend's voice. So why not record a message to your friend using a tape recorder, then mail her the cassette?

❀ *Send e-mail.* If you and your friend are both on the Internet, ask your parents for permission to e-mail your friend. Depending on what sort of Internet service you have, you and your friend may be able to create a private chat room for just the two of you. Or you may be able to use instant messaging to let each other know when you're on-line.

✿ *Write letters.* Mailing letters may seem old-fashioned if you're used to sending e-mail, but receiving an envelope in your mailbox addressed to you can be a real pick-me-up, especially if you're returning home after a not-so-great day. And by writing to your long-distance friend, you're bound to get a letter in return!

For a fun twist on a letter, make it double as a jigsaw puzzle. Write your letter on a piece of heavy cardboard. Then have an adult use scissors to cut the cardboard into a dozen or so puzzle pieces. Mail your friend the puzzle along with a note telling her that she has to assemble the puzzle before she can read your letter.

Whether you're sending a cassette, an e-mail, or a letter, keep your friend up-to-date on what's happening with you. Talk about fun things you've done and places you've gone, what's new with your family, and what you're learning in school. If she's the one who moved away, fill your friend in on the latest news about other pals and your favorite teachers and coaches. And don't forget to ask about what's going on in her life!

Special Occasions

Special occasions call for special messages. For your friend's birthday, you'll want to send a card, of course. But you might also want to send her a present. And if you don't have the money to buy her something, you can still surprise her with a poem or a drawing of the two of you. Other special occasions can include holidays and the anniversary of when the two of you started the long-distance phase of your friendship (in other words, the day you or she moved away). And then there's Friendship Day, which is August 1. Just be sure to mail your bud her card and package at least several days before the special date, to make sure she receives it in time.

Safely Making Friends On-line

Thanks to the World Wide Web, you can make friends worldwide! Whether you're interested in ballet or horseback riding, there's an on-line chat room with other people just as eager as you to discuss their favorite topics.

But while the Internet is great for meeting new people, you do have to be careful. Sometimes people will lie on the Internet. For instance, a grown-up man might pretend to be a girl your age. There's no good reason for someone to lie like that on-line. What's more, you have no way of knowing whether the person you are chatting with is telling the truth. That's why you need to follow a few dos and don'ts when you use the Internet.

☆ DO use an alias — a fake name — whenever you post messages or communicate with someone on-line. Rather than using your real name, come up with a creative nickname. For instance, if you love ballet, use the name Ballet Slippers.

☆ DON'T ever give out your real name, your phone number, your home address, your parents' work address or phone number, or the name and location of your school to anyone on-line. If a chat room or Web site requires you to provide that information, do not give the info unless you've shown the Web site to your parents first and get their OK.

☆ DO let a parent know which Web sites and chat rooms you plan to visit.

☆ DON'T agree to meet in person with anyone you've met on-line without asking a parent first. And even if you get permission, make sure that you meet the person in a public place, and that a parent is with you.

☆ DO be suspicious if an on-line pal is asking you too many questions. If she is, be sure to tell a parent.

☆ DON'T give out your Internet password to anyone except a parent.

☆ DO let a parent know immediately if you come across anything on-line, that upsets you or makes you feel uncomfortable.

☆ DON'T send any pictures to someone you've met on-line.

Practicing Good Netiquette

If you make sure not to speak with your mouth full and to say "please" and "thank you," you're practicing etiquette — a fancy way of saying good manners. The Internet has its own rules for good manners, called Netiquette. Whenever you send an e-mail or take part in a chat room, you'll make a better impression by practicing Netiquette. For instance:

☆ Don't type in all capital letters. IT IS THE EQUIVALENT OF SHOUTING AT SOMEONE.

☆ Separate paragraphs with a blank line. That makes your message easier to read.

☆ Keep it clean. Don't use any language that you wouldn't use in front of your family or teachers — for all you know, they may be in the chat room with you!

☆ Think carefully before you send anything. Keep things friendly and don't say anything you wouldn't say to a friend's face. Getting involved in an argument on the Internet is called a "flame war" — and that's the last thing you want to do!

☆ Another part of Netiquette involves the special language of the Web. On-line users have created some cool abbreviations and symbols for fun and to save typing. Try using some of these in your next e-mail or on-line chat session:

- BBL = be back later
- CUL8R = see you later
- GF = girlfriend
- IMO = in my opinion
- KIT = keep in touch
- LOL = laughing out loud
- TTFN = ta-ta for now
- TTYL = talk to you later
- WB = welcome back
- WTG = way to go
- :) or :-) = a happy face
- ;) or ;-) = a winking face
- : (or :-(= a frown

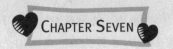

CHAPTER SEVEN

Celebrating Friendship

Friends and friendship have inspired songs and crafts throughout the centuries. There are plenty of ways you can take advantage of these friendships of the past with your own friends.

Sing-along

Your parents, your older brothers and sisters, and other members of your family or your household probably have dozens of tapes and CDs featuring songs about friendship. To make a really cool gift for a friend, why not put together a tape recording of a handful of these songs. A few suggestions:

✦ "Anytime You Need a Friend," *by Mariah Carey*

✦ "Friends," *by Elton John*

✦ "I'll Be There for You," *by the Rembrandts* (theme song from the TV series *Friends*)

- ✦ "That's What Friends Are For," *by Dionne Warwick and Friends*

- ✦ "With a Little Help from My Friends," *by the Beatles*

- ✦ "You've Got a Friend," *by James Taylor*

- ✦ "You've Got a Friend in Me," *by Randy Newman and Lyle Lovett* (theme song from the movie *Toy Story*)

Notable Quotables

Sometimes you might read words said by someone else and think, "That's exactly how I feel." You're not the only one. In fact, there are huge reference books of great quotations to help people like you find just the right words to express themselves.

Next time you want to tell a friend how much she means to you, or maybe apologize for something you did wrong, leaf through the quotations below. One of them might make the perfect birthday, thank-you, or "thinking of you" card.

* "The best friend is the one who brings out the best in me." — *20th-century U.S. inventor Henry Ford*

* "Friendship is the only cement that will ever hold the world together." — *20th-century U.S. President Woodrow Wilson*

* "Gems may be precious, but friends are priceless." — *Anonymous*

* "A good friend can live far away and still be close to your heart." — *Anonymous*

* "Make new friends, but keep the old; one is silver, and the other's gold." — *Anonymous*

* "No man is useless while he has a friend." — *19th-century Scottish writer Robert Louis Stevenson*

* "True happiness consists not in a multitude of friends, but in the worth and choice of friends." — *Anonymous*

* "What is a friend? A single soul dwelling in two bodies." — *ancient Greek philosopher Aristotle*

Friendship Wearables

Since friendships are so valuable, it's little wonder that over time people have commemorated them with jewelry. More than 300 years ago, according to legend, an Irish jeweler created a ring to represent everlasting love and eternal friendship. This ring shows two hands, one on each side of a heart. The heart always has a crown on top, which symbolizes loyalty.

More recent, and very popular, are friendship bracelets. You can make these yourself. Some are beaded, while others are made simply of yarn. Usually, though, they consist of multiple strands of thread, yarn, or beads braided together to symbolize how you and your pal are entwined together in friendship. When making a friendship bracelet for your bud, don't forget to make an identical one for yourself!

Friendship Decorations

In Japan, friendship branches are sometimes given for birthdays and anniversaries — but there's no reason why you can't give one to a friend any old time! These are especially nice to make as a way of welcoming spring. Find a tree branch that's approximately one foot long with several twigs on it. Next, cut small flower petals or blossoms out of pink construction or tissue paper and glue or tape them to the branch. (In Japan, pink blossoms stand for joy.) Then hang small charms, trinkets, or cutouts from the twigs. These charms can relate to your friend's hobbies — if she is crazy about dogs, for instance, you could hang a few pictures of dogs cut out from magazines. If possible, finish by hanging a pair of dice (or a drawing of dice), for good luck.

Although quilting has been popular since before the time of the Revolutionary War, it was especially big during the 1800s among frontier people in the United States. In frontier settlements, women from miles around would get together for quilting bees and to enjoy one another's company. Today, many of the intricately patterned quilts created at these bees hang in people's homes as artwork. Some are even displayed in museums.

One type of quilt, a friendship quilt, consists of patches of fabric embroidered with the names and birthdays of friends, along with other patches decorated to symbolize certain things about them. You can create your own version of a friendship quilt using construction paper, crayons, paints, and glitter instead of fabric. Cut out nine to twelve squares of paper, each of them the same size. These will be your patches. Then draw or paint on each patch something that stands for your friendship. If your friend's an ace soccer player, paint a soccer ball on one patch. If you admire the way she always sticks up for the unpopular kids in your class, say so on another patch. Just don't forget to leave one patch free for you to write her name! When all the patches are decorated, glue them in rows of three on a piece of cardboard. Now your friend will have her very own friendship quilt!

Other Friendship Gifts

In England during the late 1800s, friendship balls became a trend. These are round ornaments that open up to hold little gifts or trinkets. In the olden days, a woman would give a ball to her friend on a special occasion, such as her wedding. Then the friend would return the ball to her months or years later on another special occasion, such as a birthday.

You can make your own friendship ball from a large hollow foam or plastic ball found in a craft shop. Have an adult slice the ball in half for you. Then decorate the outside using paint, colored paper, and ribbons — the fancier the better. As for the inside, fill it with tiny toys, candies, or even a small note in which you tell your friend why you like her so much. Then surprise your bud with the ball. Make sure you explain that the ball is supposed to pass back and forth between the two of you, to symbolize the never-ending circle of your friendship.

Not all gifts are objects. A gift can also be a special event, such as a Japanese friendship tea. This event is a way of showing your friend just how special she is to you. Once you get permission from a parent, give your bud a handwritten invitation to a tea in her honor. Then with a grown-up's help, plan a special afternoon snack for her. Prepare her favorite cake, cookies, or fruit, arranging everything nicely on the table. Fold the napkins into whatever fancy shapes you can, and write out place cards, even though your friend is the only guest. You may even want to present her with a poem or a card in which you tell her just how special she is to you.

Forever Friends

Theres's nothing more valuable than a friend. Whether you want to make a new friend, heal a broken friendship, or simply show a bud how much she means to you, you can do it with this book, which has offered advice, suggestions, and inspiration. Then all you have to do is enjoy and appreciate the friendships that you have!